THE EARTHQUAKE IN HAITI

Essential Events

THE EARTHQUAKE IN HAITI

BY ANNE LIES

Content Consultant
Eloy Nuñez, PhD
emergency management consultant
retired lieutenant, Miami-Dade Police Department

ABDO
Publishing Company

CREDITS

Published by ABDO Publishing Company, 8000 West 78th Street, Edina, Minnesota 55439. Copyright © 2011 by Abdo Consulting Group, Inc. International copyrights reserved in all countries. No part of this book may be reproduced in any form without written permission from the publisher. The Essential Library™ is a trademark and logo of ABDO Publishing Company.

Printed in the United States of America,
North Mankato, Minnesota
062010
092010

 THIS BOOK CONTAINS AT LEAST 10% RECYCLED MATERIALS.

Editor: Rebecca Rowell
Copy Editor: David Johnstone
Interior Design and Production: Becky Daum
Cover Design: Kazuko Collins

Library of Congress Cataloging-in-Publication Data
Lies, Anne, 1968-
  The earthquake in Haiti / Anne Lies.
      p. cm. — (Essential events)
  Includes bibliographical references and index.
  ISBN 978-1-61613-682-6
  1. Haiti Earthquake, Haiti, 2010—Juvenile literature. I. Title.
  F1928.2.L54 2011
  972.94'073—dc22

                                  2010019653

TABLE OF CONTENTS

A beach on Haiti

New Year's Hopes

As 2009 drew to a close, Haitians looked forward to 2010—it was going to be a better year for Haiti. After 16 months of effort, it looked as though the tropical country was mostly recovered from a devastating hurricane season in the summer of 2008. In less than one month that year, the island had been ravaged by four violent storms, three of which were hurricanes. More than 800 people died in those storms, and the desperately poor country suffered tremendous damage to buildings, roads, and crops.

Haiti is the poorest country in the Western Hemisphere. The average income there is the equivalent of about $660 per year. An outpouring of international support in the fall of 2008 helped the nation recover and rebuild. In 2009, the government raised the minimum wage from 70 to 200 gourdes per day, which is an increase from about $1.30 to $5.00 per day. With storm recovery well on its way, and 2009 mercifully free of other hurricanes and natural disasters, 2010 was looking brighter.

A Shift of Plates

The Caribbean, the area of ocean and islands between the northernmost tip of South America and the Gulf of Mexico, is famous for

Season of Sadness

The 2008 hurricane season left Haiti in shambles. In addition to killing 800 people, the relentless storms ruined approximately 60 percent of the nation's crops and left some towns virtually uninhabitable. One million people were left homeless. The four huge storms began on August 16, when Tropical Storm Fay made landfall on Haiti. In the next three weeks, Fay was followed by hurricanes Gustav, Hanna, and Ike.

What Is in a Name?

Haiti's official name is the Republic of Haiti (République d'Haïti in French, and Republik d'Ayiti in Creole). When the Spaniards landed on the island of Hispaniola, it was inhabited by an indigenous tribe called the Taino. The name Haiti comes from the Taino word *ayti* (or *hayti*), which means "mountainous land." With five major mountain ranges in a country roughly the size of the state of Maryland, it is an appropriate name.

its hurricanes. It is also famous for its earthquakes. Geologists have long known that the island of Hispaniola, home to Haiti and the Dominican Republic, is situated atop two fault lines—meeting points for the massive tectonic plates that form the crust of Earth. On January 12, 2010, one of those plates would shift.

With an estimated 9 million people, Haiti is one of the most densely populated countries in the world. The government spends little money on education. Only about half of Haitians can read, and only about 65 percent of children attend grade school. Even fewer, about 10 percent, reach high school before they drop out to find work to support themselves or their families.

On the afternoon of Tuesday, January 12, children fortunate enough to go to school were finishing classes for the day. In the capital city of Port-au-Prince, fifth-grader Madjany Mouscardy was relaxing after school with her *Hannah Montana* computer game. Other students, such as seventh-grader Maximillien François, were in their schoolyards playing soccer, a favorite sport in Haiti. Still others had work to do before they could have fun. Twelve-year-old Lemark Aristide was in his bedroom doing homework and listening to his father rock his baby brother to sleep in the next room. Garvey Fils-Amie, 11, was sitting outside his house. A tutor was helping him with his lessons. January is a dry season in Haiti, so there was very little chance that rain would interrupt their work that afternoon.

CARNIVAL PLANS

About 25 miles (39 km) across the Tiburon

One Island, Two Cultures

Haiti is situated on the western third of the island of Hispaniola. The Dominican Republic makes up the other two thirds. Christopher Columbus claimed the island for Spain in 1492, and for the next 50 years, the eastern side, Santo Domingo, was a prosperous colony. It had rich gold mines and served as Spain's operating base in the New World. Once the island's gold mines were exhausted, Spanish settlers moved on to Mexico, and Santo Domingo was neglected.

Santo Domingo declared independence from Spain in 1821, but it was taken over by Haiti for 22 years. It won independence as the Dominican Republic in 1844. The Dominican Republic suffered under dictators and unstable governments. From 1930 to 1961, the nation was ruled by Rafael Trujillo, a brutal dictator who fostered anti-Haitian prejudice. In 1937, he ordered the massacre of thousands of Haitian migrants. He was assassinated in 1961.

The Dominican Republic's current president is Leonel Fernández. He was first elected in 1996. He was elected again in 2004 and a third time in 2008. The Dominican Republic is a popular tourist destination, and tourism is an important part of the country's economy.

Haitians celebrate carnival in Jacmel.

Peninsula from Port-au-Prince, the city of Jacmel
was preparing for the biggest party of the year.
Carnival, which is celebrated in Haiti every year in
February or March, is an exuberant and colorful
midwinter festival that draws visitors from near and
far. Although it is just as poor as the rest of Haiti,
Jacmel is a beautiful, old city, with brightly colored
buildings that face down a hillside toward the
turquoise ocean. It is considered the cultural capital
of Haiti. It is also known as a city of artists, many of
whom make their living creating costumes and giant
papier-mâché masks for Jacmel's famous carnival
parade. With the annual celebration only a few weeks

away, most of the masks were finished, just waiting to be shown off.

TWILIGHT TREMOR

At 4:53 p.m., everything changed. The tectonic plates along the Enriquillo-Plantain Garden Fault ground against one another, creating an earthquake of horrible force. The bright walls of Jacmel began to shake as the ground beneath them rocked. At first, many people did not realize what was happening. Frightened, many of them ran out of their houses and into the streets of the town, which probably saved their lives. Many of those who stayed inside buildings were killed when the walls collapsed on them. Others were alive but trapped under heavy blocks of concrete and piles of rubble. Carnival was about to become a season of mourning as the country suffered its worst catastrophe yet.

In Port-au-Prince, Madjany Mouscardy looked up from her

Carnival

In Christian traditions, Lent is a holy season that begins on Ash Wednesday and lasts for 40 days in preparation for the Easter holiday. In many parts of the Caribbean, the days just ahead of Lent are marked by carnival holidays, which give people a chance to celebrate one last time before the more somber season of fasting and prayer begins. Carnival usually involves parades or street parties, and participants often dress in bright costumes and masks for the festivities. Similar celebrations take place in the United States. The city of New Orleans, Louisiana, is famous for its carnival season, which ends with Mardi Gras, or Fat Tuesday.

computer to see the walls of the room she was in "shaking like a swing."[1] Moments later, she fell through a hole from the second story of the building and was trapped under bricks and rubble. Max François was too close to a wall of his school building when the quake hit. The wall fell on him, crushing his leg and trapping him in fright and confusion.

The walls of Lemark Aristide's bedroom collapsed on him, pinning his legs. In the next room, his father and baby brother were also trapped. Garvey Fils-Amie's house crumbled as he sat in safety outside. His mother did not get out in time. Though he tried, Garvey was not able to help her, and she died inside.

In 40 seconds, the 7.0 earthquake of January 12, 2010, all but destroyed Haiti. Ultimately, 230,000 people would die, and 1.5 million would be homeless as a result of the disaster. The promise of a better year for Haiti would not become reality in 2010. In fact, the nightmare was only beginning.

In the aftermath of the earthquake in Haiti, people searched through the rubble of buildings hoping to find survivors.

The small nation of Haiti has had a long and troubled history.

HAITI'S EARLY HISTORY

The earthquake of January 12, 2010, devastated the nation of Haiti. It was not the strongest or farthest reaching earthquake ever to occur, but it impacted Haiti far worse than similar quakes in other parts of the world. To understand why this earthquake caused such destruction and misery, it is necessary to understand Haiti's extreme poverty. This requires understanding Haiti's history.

DISCOVERY

Haiti is located on the island of Hispaniola in the tropical waters of the Caribbean Sea. The first European to see the island was Christopher Columbus. On December 5, 1492, he spotted it from the deck of the *Santa Maria*. Columbus claimed the island for the king of Spain, naming it *La Isla Española*, "the Spanish Island." The name was later Anglicized, or converted to English, as Hispaniola. The Spaniards who settled on the island mostly wanted gold. They enslaved huge numbers of the native Taino people, forcing them to mine the precious metal. Many of the slaves died from diseases that came with the Europeans. Many more died from brutal treatment, and by the late 1500s, the native tribes were all but wiped out.

Importing Illness

The European explorers landing in the New World brought more with them than the contents of their ships. They also brought Old World illnesses, such as smallpox. Smallpox is highly contagious and often fatal. While the Europeans had been exposed to and developed some resistance to the disease, new peoples they encountered had no such immunity. The first recorded outbreak of smallpox in the Americas was in 1507 on Hispaniola. Some 200,000 of the island's native people died of smallpox brought by Spanish settlers.

Slavery is part of Haiti's history.

More Spaniards arrived in the colony, which was called Santo Domingo. They soon discovered that Hispaniola's tropical climate was perfect for growing sugarcane. By 1506, they were growing the valuable crop. The sugarcane plantations increased the need for workers, but the native slaves were dying off. In 1510, King Ferdinand of Spain began sending ships filled with enslaved Africans to the colony to work in the mines and on the plantations.

PIRATES OF THE CARIBBEAN

While the Spaniards settled mostly on the eastern side of the island, French and English pirates and buccaneers began to establish bases on the western side. From there, it was easy to attack Spanish ships bringing gold and silver to Spain. It was such a good arrangement that some of the French buccaneers made permanent settlements. Some established plantations to grow valuable crops, such as tobacco and sugarcane. By 1640, they had forced out their English rivals, and within a few years, the western side of Hispaniola was claimed by King Louis XIII of France. Taking their cue from Spain, the French called the colony Saint-Domingue. In 1697, the Treaty of Ryswick officially divided the island between Spain and France.

By the end of the eighteenth century, Saint-Domingue was an extremely successful and profitable colony for France. It was responsible for two thirds of all France's overseas trade. In 1789, the colony exported enough sugar, cotton, indigo, coffee, cacao, and tobacco to fill more than 4,000 ships.

Saint-Domingue was the world's largest sugar producer, supplying nearly 75 percent of the world's sugar trade. To maintain this level of production as profitably as possible required so much slave labor that the number of slaves in Saint-Domingue far outnumbered the number of free people. According to census figures, in 1687, the colony had a population of 8,000. White European colonists totaled 4,500; the rest were slaves. By 1791, the population had exploded to 520,000: 40,000 whites, 30,000 free people of color, and 450,000 African slaves.

Social Classes

The population of Saint-Domingue was divided into four groups. The *grands blancs*, or greater whites, were white colonists who were either European settlers or descendants of Europeans. They were the wealthiest class, and they controlled the government. Another class of whites was the *petits blancs,* or lesser whites. These were poor laborers. The next group, the *Affranchis,* consisted of free people of color. Some of the members of this class were freed slaves. Many were people of mixed race, whose fathers were white and whose mothers were African slaves. The largest class was made up of African slaves.

Many free people of color were well-educated merchants and business owners. Some were quite wealthy, with plantations and slaves of their own. Many adopted the European customs and culture of the white colonists. They tried to distance themselves as much as they could from the African slave culture. They did not, however, have the same rights and political power as the white colonists.

CHANGING
FORTUNES

In the 1700s, ideas such as democratic governments and liberty captured the imaginations of men in Europe and the Americas. The American Revolution (1775–1783) broke the

Toussaint L'Ouverture

Toussaint L'Ouverture was born into slavery in Bréda, Saint-Domingue, in 1743. His given name was François Dominique Toussaint. He was educated and intelligent. His master legally freed him in 1777. When the slave revolt of 1791 broke out, Toussaint helped his former master escape before joining the fight against plantation owners. By 1793, he was a leader of the revolutionaries. He adopted the name L'Ouverture, which means "the opening" in French. That year, France and Spain went to war. L'Ouverture sided with Spain against France. In 1794, France declared its slaves free. L'Ouverture then sided with the French to drive out British and Spanish forces.

L'Ouverture worked to repair the economy of Saint-Domingue. He convinced some white plantation owners to return and help rebuild the colony. He also made sure former slaves were treated fairly and paid for their work.

By 1801, L'Ouverture had gained control of all of Hispaniola. He wrote a new constitution and named himself governor-general for life, but he did not declare independence from France. In an attempt to take control of its colony, France kidnapped L'Ouverture. He was imprisoned in Fort-de-Joux in France. He died there in 1803.

bonds of British colonial rule, creating the United States of America. The French Revolution of 1789 overturned that country's royal rule. Beginning two years later, French control of Saint-Domingue would be broken by the only successful slave revolt in history.

Toussaint L'Ouverture, Jean-Jacques Dessalines, and Henry Christophe were former slaves who rose to lead the revolution. L'Ouverture was undoubtedly inspired by the French and American revolutions and their concepts of freedom. He was devoted to the cause of ending slavery in the colony and hoped to maintain Saint-Domingue's profitable business. In 1801, L'Ouverture conquered Santo Domingo and began overseeing the entire island. He claimed allegiance to France but was most devoted to his people. France sent troops to the island to gain control and capture L'Ouverture. The Haitian was arrested and taken to France, where he died imprisoned in a dungeon before the revolutionaries' victory.

The revolution lasted for more than 12 years. When it was over, on January 1, 1804, Dessalines declared the new republic would be called by its ancient name: Haiti. Its freedom was hard won, and the country lay in ruins. The plantations were destroyed, and their white owners who did not escape were killed. L'Ouverture's vision for the new republic's economy was impossible.

HAITI'S NEW ECONOMY

The Haitian revolution created a new type of economy in the country. The huge plantations had been destroyed and were replaced with small, family-owned properties. Former slaves grew food for their families on their own land. They could sell any extra food to others.

The United States would have been a logical trading partner, but as a nation still using African slave labor, it was not comfortable with the new black republic. Even if that had not been the case, Haiti no longer had an economy based on selling goods to other countries. It now had a smaller, internal economy. For fear of being pushed back into slavery, the new government made it illegal for foreigners to own land in Haiti.

Ripples of the Revolution

The United States was affected by Haiti's successful revolution. With the defeat of the French forces in Saint-Domingue, French leader Napoleon Bonaparte's hopes for an empire in the New World were crushed. He also needed to finance his war efforts in Europe. As a result, in 1803, he offered the massive French territory of Louisiana to the United States. For less than three cents per acre, the Louisiana Purchase doubled the size of the United States.

CHAOS AT THE TOP

Adding to its other difficulties, Haiti's leadership was unstable. The leadership class was made up of a small number of mixed-race and light-skinned Haitians. These were the wealthiest people in the country. They spoke French and continued to identify with their French heritage. They treated the Creole-speaking class of darker-skinned former slaves as peasants. Between 1843 and 1915, Haiti had 22 presidents. All but one of them were assassinated or forced out of office. All had sought political power to make themselves—and their supporters—rich.

The destruction of the revolution, the crushing debt to France, and government corruption led to most of Haiti's people being poor. These factors left little possibility for anything else. In addition, the racial and cultural divide between the light-skinned elites and the dark-skinned majority has continued to this day.

Today, a statue honoring Toussaint L'Ouverture stands in Port-Au-Prince.

The Panama Canal

Haiti in the Twentieth Century

After the revolution for independence from France, Haiti became isolated from the rest of the world. That does not mean the rest of the world lost interest in Haiti. In particular, the United States kept a close eye on the tropical republic. Only approximately 700 miles (1,127 km) from Florida, Haiti's political unrest and almost continuous turnover of leadership concerned the U.S. government. In 1888, U.S. Assistant Secretary of State Alvey A. Adee called Haiti "a public nuisance at our doors."[1] With the opening of the Panama Canal in 1914, the United States had even more interest in keeping stability in the Caribbean.

On July 28, 1915, the U.S. Marines invaded Haiti. Officially, the goal was to restore and maintain order in Haiti. The United States took political and financial control of the country. A new constitution was introduced, and for the first time since the revolution, foreigners were allowed to own land in Haiti. There were protests and rebellions, some of which were put down violently.

The United States occupied Haiti until 1934. In that 19-year span, there were some positive developments, such as the building of roads, bridges, health clinics, and sewer systems. Those improvements

The Panama Canal

Haiti is the gateway to the Caribbean Sea, a popular waterway for U.S. vessels. The Panama Canal is a 40-mile (64-km) canal that connects the Atlantic Ocean to the Pacific Ocean via the Caribbean Sea. The canal was built by the United States to create an easier way to sail ships from the East Coast of the United States to the West Coast. Without it, ships had to sail all the way around Cape Horn, the southern tip of South America. The Panama Canal opened in 1914.

did not have a lasting effect on Haiti's poverty or on its political system, however. One Haitian scholar, Michel-Rolf Trouillot, claims the occupation "worsened all of Haiti's structural ills . . . America's military and political interventions in Haiti have never been backed by sufficiently sustained or vigorous efforts to ease the country's crippling poverty."[2] The occupation did, however, centralize much of Haiti's commerce in the Port-au-Prince area.

The Bloody Rule of the Duvaliers

After the Americans left in 1934, Haiti lapsed into unstable government. By the mid-1950s, any improvements that the U.S. occupation had put in place were largely gone. Roads and bridges had fallen into ruin, and public health clinics were in decline. In 1957, François "Papa Doc" Duvalier was elected president. His 14-year term in power was unusually long. It was also unusually brutal.

Duvalier was a doctor who had served as minister of Labor and director general of the Public Health Service under President Dumarsais Estimé. Estimé had been removed from office by the military after he tried to extend his term. After that, Duvalier

Francois "Papa Doc" Duvalier

waited for his chance to get back into political office. He ran for president by stoking the fires of racial tension, promising to put an end to the rule of the elites. He appealed to the middle and poorer classes by emphasizing Haiti's African heritage.

After a failed attempt to overthrow him in 1958, Duvalier created a private militia of his own guards to carry out murders and terrorize anyone who opposed him. Citizens called them the *Tonton Macoutes*, which means "bogeymen" in Creole. Duvalier openly declared that labor unions and other organizations that opposed him would be crushed. "All popular movements," he said, "will be repressed with utmost rigor [strictness]. The repression will be total, inflexible, and inexorable [unstoppable]."[3]

In 1964, Duvalier named himself president for life. He also gave himself the right to choose his own successor. He was acting more like a king than a president. He portrayed himself as a defender of the working class, yet his presidency only helped a small group of the middle class who supported him. Ultimately, he did nothing to address the poverty of his people, and he only strengthened the color divide in Haiti.

In 1971, Duvalier announced that his son, Jean-Claude, would take his place as president. When the elder Duvalier died that spring, the 19-year-old Jean-Claude was made the next president for life. The people called him "Baby Doc" and, like his father, he ruled by fear and intimidation.

Frightening Figures

The name *Tonton Macoutes* comes from a Haitian children's legend. At Christmastime, good children got gifts from *Tonton Noël*, "Uncle Christmas." Children who were bad were taken away by *Tonton Macoute*, or "Uncle Knapsack." François Duvalier's brutal and murderous guards got the name because their victims would often disappear, never to be seen again.

Tonton Macoutes *marched in Port-Au-Prince*
in support of Papa Doc in 1970.

During Papa Doc's rule, many Haitians,
particularly professionals such as doctors, lawyers,
and teachers, escaped the country. By the mid–
1960s, an estimated 80 percent of Haitian
professionals had relocated. Baby Doc's rise to power
set off a new wave of departures. By 1976, there were
150,000 Haitians living in New York City alone.

Baby Doc made efforts to raise Haiti's profile
in the international community. In doing so, he

managed to reinstate some of the international aid money that had been taken away while his father was in power. Some tourism also returned to the island nation. On the outside, Haiti seemed to have improved, but very little had changed inside the country.

The Duvaliers were cruel dictators. It is estimated that they ordered the deaths of some 40,000 Haitians during their regimes. By the mid-1980s, living conditions in Haiti had become so bad that the people began to revolt, even though

---

Vodou

There is an old saying that Haiti is 80 percent Catholic and 100 percent vodou. Catholicism and vodou (sometimes spelled *voodoo*) are the two national religions of Haiti. The name vodou comes from the Fon language of slaves brought from Dahomey (now the African country of Benin). The word means "god" or "spirit." One basic belief of vodou is that humans and spirits, or *loa*, can interact with one another through rituals and ceremonies. Followers are faithful to a god named Bondje. The name comes from the French words *bon Dieu*, which mean "good God."

Vodou spirits and Catholic saints can seem very similar. Before the revolution, many slaves in the colony of Saint-Domingue were forbidden to practice vodou. To hide their rituals from their Catholic masters, slaves would use images of saints.

Many people think of vodou as a religion of sorcery and evil. Hollywood movies and other media often portray it as something exotic, but it is really just an ordinary part of Haitian life and belief. According to Claudine Michel, a professor of Black Studies at the University of California, Santa Barbara, "People turn to the spirits and their ancestors to secure a better life for themselves and their community. . . ."[4] In 2003, Jean-Bertrand Aristide officially declared vodou a national religion of Haiti.

they feared the powerful *Tonton Macoutes*. By 1986, Baby Doc and his guards could no longer silence the protesters. Protesters demanded that Baby Doc step down. On February 7, he and his family fled the country and went to France.

Haitians were optimistic that the harsh government would improve after Baby Doc left. Although the vast majority of Haitians suffered under the Duvaliers, some citizens and officials preferred that the government system stay the same. When Baby Doc fled Haiti, the military grabbed control of the government. Again, very little changed. The people of Haiti were desperate for their government to bring about effective change.

Far from Home

Sometimes, the Haitian communities in other countries are referred to as the Haitian diaspora. A diaspora can be any group of people who has settled far from its ancestral homeland. In the United States, there are large Haitian communities in Florida and New York. Other Haitian communities can be found in Canada, Guadeloupe, France, French Guiana, the Bahamas, Cuba, and Martinique.

ARISTIDE'S NEW HOPE

Four more years of uncertainty and bloodshed followed Baby Doc's departure to France. In 1990, however, it looked as though true reform might happen. On December 16, Jean-Bertrand Aristide became the first freely and democratically elected president of Haiti. Aristide was a Catholic priest who had massive popular support. He won the election in a landslide with promises to reform Haiti's corrupt government and unfair economic system. He would remain in office for less than one year.

On September 30, 1991, a military coup d'état, or takeover, forced Aristide out. In the eight months since his inauguration, he had made attempts to cut corruption in the military and to control the drug trafficking in Haiti. He had also tried to create income for his reforms by taxing the wealthy. The elites did not want to see these kinds of changes. They pressured Raoul Cédras, the chief of staff of Aristide's army, to take over the government. Aristide had no choice but to flee the country.

Haiti was forced into another dictatorship. Newspapers and radio stations that spoke out against the government were shut down. People who

Jean-Claude "Baby Doc" Duvalier

protested were jailed, and many were tortured and killed. Thousands of Haitians fled, setting sail for the United States in small boats. Those who could prove their lives were in danger in Haiti were allowed to stay in the United States. Most were sent back. Once they returned to Haiti, they faced beatings and arrest for trying to escape. Some were killed.

With endorsement by the United Nations (UN) and the help of the U.S. military, Aristide was restored to power in October 1994. He took some important steps toward stabilizing Haiti, such as purging the army of senior officers who had been part of the coup d'état, but he was not able to make lasting changes to his nation's economic and political systems. Though his original term had been interrupted by the coup, he was required by law to step down when it was over.

In 1995, René Préval was elected president of Haiti. He had been prime minister under Aristide before the coup. Many considered this to be the first time in Haiti's history that government control was peacefully and democratically passed from one president to another in a fair election. Others believed Aristide actually was the power behind Préval's election and presidency.

In 2001, Aristide was elected again. The elections were protested. Over the next three years, Aristide was accused of misusing government funds and terrorizing his opponents. By 2004, many of the people who were once his strongest supporters believed he was no better than any other corrupt president before him. In the face of a bitter and bloody revolt, Aristide left Haiti again in 2004. He went into exile in South Africa, and Préval again became president of Haiti.

Newly sworn-in Haitian president René Préval, right, is embraced by former president Jean-Bertrand Aristide in February 1996.

Slum housing on the outskirts of Port-au-Prince, Haiti

Haiti's Challenges

When Préval was elected president of Haiti again in 2006, he faced a nation that was as poor as it had ever been. Guiding his country out of its problems will be a challenge. Even before the January 2010 earthquake, many experts doubted it was possible given Haiti's history and resources.

POVERTY

Haiti's poverty is staggering. Though some Haitians grow coffee and sugar for export, most of the country's agriculture is subsistence farming. Farmers raise enough food for their families, with perhaps a little extra to sell at local markets. Some 70 percent of the population of approximately 9 million is officially unemployed. Only about 20,000 people work in U.S.-owned factories making goods such as electronics, clothing, and toys for export.

Many thousands of Haitians live outside their homeland. According to U.S. census figures, there are more than 750,000 Haitians in the United States. Many of them send money to family members living in Haiti. It is estimated that $1.5 to $1.8 billion is sent to Haiti yearly through these

Subsistence Farming

Subsistence farmers work to provide food for local use, not for export. In Haiti, farmers grow a variety of crops, including bananas, plantains, coffee, sugarcane, and sisal, a plant whose fiber is used for twine and other products. These crops tend to provide farmers with much-needed revenue. Other crops are grown for sale or simply to be consumed on the farm. These include beans, corn, rice, and fruit.

Haitian farmers face several challenges. Lack of passable roads hampers transportation between farms and markets where products are sold. Farmers also lack current mechanization and technology. In addition, irrigation systems, which are crucial to farming success, are inconsistent.

Haiti relied on food donations long before the 2010 earthquake.

remittances—roughly half of Haiti's entire national income. Without that money, some Haitians would not be able to survive at all.

Such extreme poverty brings other problems. Port-au-Prince is a haven for international crime. It is a well-known highway for illegal drugs into the United States. Haiti is also known for trafficking something else: children. It is estimated that as many as 300,000 Haitian children are working as *restaveks*. These are Haitian children in poor families sent to be live-in domestic helpers for other families.

The idea is that the new family will provide a better future for the child than his or her own family. But *restaveks* often live in slavelike conditions. Many are from rural areas and are sent by their poor families to live with wealthier families in cities as servants. Many families agree to let a child go because they feel their poverty leaves them with no other choice.

PUBLIC SERVICES

Public services in Haiti are unstable. In 2000, Haiti's transportation system had just over 4,000 miles (6,437 km) of paved roads. By contrast, the Dominican Republic has more than 19,000 miles (30,578 km). The 2010 earthquake hit this vulnerable system while the country was still trying to recover from the damage caused by the hurricanes of 2008.

Utilities are also an issue. As few as one in nine people has reliable electricity. In addition, few homes have indoor plumbing, and clean drinking water is scarce for many.

Tap-Taps

Public transportation in Haiti consists of brightly colored vans, buses, and trucks called "tap-taps." They operate more like taxis than buses. They are privately owned and follow a certain route, but they do not follow a particular schedule. The name comes from the signal that riders give when they want to get out—a sharp "tap-tap" on the side of the vehicle.

Haiti's lack of public health services has been a long-standing issue for the nation. Poor sanitation means that Haiti has some of the highest rates of disease in the world. It is estimated that more than 200,000 Haitians suffer from HIV and AIDS. Proper nutrition is another problem. Child malnutrition is a serious issue, especially in rural areas. The nongovernmental organization Médecins Sans Frontières (MSF), or Doctors Without Borders, has been operating in Haiti since 1991. Even with the organization's help, the public health system is too weak to meet the country's needs.

Mudslides

Deforestation is a huge problem in Haiti. Without trees to hold the soil in place, the country's rainy season turns into a muddy season, with tragic results. In 2004, Hurricane Jeanne hit Haiti. More than 3,000 people were killed. Almost all of them died in flooding and mudslides in Gonaives, a city in northern Haiti. Some 250,000 were left homeless.

Environmental Concerns

When the first European explorers arrived on Hispaniola, they were amazed by the island's beauty. In particular, it was covered with forests. In the centuries of colonial rule, those forests were cut down to clear fields for sugarcane and other crops. Deforestation has been worse in Haiti than in the Dominican Republic.

The slopes of Massif de la Selle mountain range above Jacmel, Haiti, were once covered with pine, cedar, and juniper trees. In 2003, they were nearing complete deforestation.

Today, while the Dominican Republic still has about 28 percent of its original tree cover, Haiti only has about 1 percent.

Deforestation is a problem, not only for the trees, but also for the farmers trying to produce food. Lack of tree cover contributes to soil erosion. Nutrient-rich topsoil washes away with every rain, so less fertile soil is left for growing crops. During the rainy season, dangerous mudslides are common. What little forest Haiti has left is still being cut down. The wood is used to make charcoal, which is the main source of cooking fuel in Haiti.

RACE AND CLASS DIVISION

One long-running problem that has caused so much of Haiti's political instability is the huge divide between its rich and poor citizens. This parallels a class divide among lighter- and darker-skinned people. The light-skinned and nonblack populations are wealthier and have more influence in government.

In addition, there is also a divide between the urban population and those who live in rural areas, where the poverty is worse. Over the years, more and more of Haiti's poor have flooded into Port-au-Prince, the nation's capital. There, they hope to find jobs and other opportunities. The city's population has swelled to about 3 million, nearly one-third of the nation's entire population. The huge slums of Port-au-Prince continue to grow. The strain on the city's services is tremendous, and there is very little of the national budget left over for the people living outside the capital city. The wealthy live in suburbs higher up in the mountains around Port-au-Prince.

Pétionville is one such place. High above the tin-roofed shacks that line the hills around Port-au-Prince, Pétionville enjoys a cooler, breezier climate and a far higher standard of living. But even this privileged town has seen the effects of the corrupt systems in Haiti. In 2008, a Pétionville school building collapsed, killing almost 100 people. At that time, the mayor of Port-au-Prince claimed that 60 percent of the buildings were so badly constructed that they were not safe. The 2010 earthquake proved him right.

RECENT IMPROVEMENTS

Change in Haiti has been slow, but it has been for the better. Since 2004, the UN has had a stabilization

Haiti's Poverty

Poverty is a way of life for thousands of Haitians. That poverty was highlighted when the earthquake destroyed the nation's capital in January 2010. Haiti is the poorest country in the Western Hemisphere. The economic struggles of the nation ultimately affect its citizens. The Micah Project is a nonprofit organization committed to helping Haitian children, many of whom are struggling to survive, get their basic needs met, and obtain an education. The Micah Project reports the following statistics about Haiti:

- *The unemployment rate is over 80%.*
- *More than half of Haitians live on less than a dollar a day.*
- *There are few paved roads, an inadequate supply of potable water, minimal utilities, and depleted forests.*
- *About 60% of the population lives in abject poverty.*
- *Less than 20% of Haitians age 15 and over can read and write.*
- *Fewer than 75% of children attend school.*
- *40% of the Haitian population does not have access to primary health care.*
- *One in twenty Haitians is infected with HIV/AIDS and there are 150,000 AIDS orphans.*[1]

Félix Morisseau-Leroy

Félix Morisseau-Leroy was a Haitian poet and playwright. He was one of the first people to write professionally using Haitian Creole instead of French. He believed it was important for Haitians to be able to enjoy literature in their own language. He defied rules of social class by working to show that Creole was just as valuable a language as French. Due in part to Morisseau-Leroy's efforts, in 1991, Jean-Bertrand Aristide declared Creole to be an official language of Haiti.

mission in Haiti (called MINUSTAH, from the French name, Mission des Nations Unies pour la Stabilisation en Haïti). The mission's original role was to restore order after Aristides's exile. It was meant to strengthen Haiti's system of law enforcement, restore government stability, and protect human rights. Though the mission has been accused at times of using violence and heavy-handed control tactics, it has made progress in training police and maintaining the rule of law.

As a UN special envoy to Haiti, former U.S. president Bill Clinton has been working closely with President Préval to forge a new economic plan for Haiti. The Haitian economy has seen small but steady growth since 2006. What remains to be seen is whether that growth can survive the events of 2010.

Many children are forced to leave their homes in the countryside to work doing such things as selling snacks to bus passengers in the cities.

A seismograph registers earthquake data.

How Earthquakes Work

The earthquake that struck Haiti in January 2010 was incredibly destructive. But most earthquakes are not as devastating. In fact, the earth experiences earthquakes every day; most are so small that no one ever feels the tremors they cause.

The earth's crust, or top layer, is made up of unsteady tectonic plates that are constantly moving against one another. The edges of the plates meet at faults. When the plates shift along those faults, earthquakes occur. The edges of the plates are not smooth, so they catch on one another and get stuck, but the plates continue to move. Over time, that movement stores up energy so that when the edges finally become "unstuck" the shift can be sudden, and sometimes violent. The released energy radiates out in all directions from the fault, just like ripples in water when a pebble breaks the surface of a pond. The waves of energy move through the earth, upward toward the surface. Once the waves reach the surface, they cause the tremors and shaking that can do anything from rattling dishes to destroying whole cities.

Unlike the Haitian earthquake, the vast majority of earthquakes are

Annual Earthquakes

Earth's tectonic plates are always on the move. According to the U.S. Geological Survey Earthquake Hazards Program, the planet experiences millions of earthquakes every year. Many go undetected because their magnitudes are so small or they occur in remote areas. As the number of seismographs in use increases, more of these earthquakes will be located.

not strong enough to be felt on the planet's surface. The U.S. Geological Survey (USGS) Earthquake Hazards Program is dedicated to seismology, the science of earthquakes, and tracks this activity. According to USGS estimates, there are 1,300,000 microquakes every year worldwide. That is more than 3,500 earthquakes every day.

One Size Does Not Fit All

The magnitude, or size, of an earthquake is usually discussed using a scale from 1 to 10. Seismic waves, which transmit the energy released by an earthquake, are recorded using a device called a seismograph. The sizes of the waves are used to determine an earthquake's magnitude. Generally, quakes with magnitudes of less than 3 cannot be felt by people. Magnitudes greater than 5 can be destructive. A magnitude 10 earthquake has never been recorded. The USGS notes, "The simple truth is that there are no known faults capable of generating a magnitude 10 or larger 'mega-quake.'"[1]

Magnitude only tells part of an earthquake's story. Other factors affect how destructive a quake turns out to be. One factor is depth. The farther below the surface of the earth a quake occurs—the hypocenter—the less intense the tremors are on the surface because they have farther to travel to reach the surface.

Another factor is the number of people living in the area of an earthquake. The greater the population, the more people are likely to be hurt, and the more damage there is likely to be to buildings and infrastructure.

THE HAITI EARTHQUAKE

When thinking about the 2010 Haiti earthquake, it is important to consider several

Measuring Earthquakes

Earthquake size is determined using several different scales. The best known is the Richter (pronounced RICK-ter) magnitude scale. It was developed in 1935 by Charles F. Richter at the California Institute of Technology:

- 2.0–2.9: micro—cannot be felt but are recorded on seismographs.
- 3.0–3.9: minor—usually no damage.
- 4.0–4.9: light—noticeable shaking, but usually no serious damage.
- 5.0–5.9: moderate—damages even well-built structures over small areas.
- 6.0–6.9: strong—can cause serious damage up to 100 miles (161 km) from the epicenter.
- 7.0–7.9: major—severe damage over larger areas, even to well-built structures.
- 8.0+: great—severe damage, even total destruction up to several hundred miles from the epicenter.

An increase of one whole number on the scale increases the strength about 31 times. Small-magnitude earthquakes take place daily. In an average year, there are 17 major and one great quake worldwide.

The moment magnitude scale also measures earthquakes. Its numbers coincide with the Richter scale, but it is more accurate for measuring quakes with magnitudes greater than 7.0.

The earthquake in Haiti destroyed Port-au-Prince, the nation's capital.

factors. First, the island of Hispaniola straddles three tectonic plates: the North America Plate, the Caribbean Plate, and, in between them, the Gonâve Platelet. Along the edges of the platelet run the Septentrional Fault in northern Haiti and the Enriquillo-Plantain Garden Fault in southern Haiti. Plates will move several millimeters a year, but the Enriquillo-Plantain Garden Fault had not had any earthquake activity for more than a century. In other words, the plates had been building up pressure for about 150 years, so when they finally became unstuck, the movement was strong and violent.

To make matters worse, the hypocenter of the quake was quite shallow—only about eight miles (13 km) below the surface. What made this quake particularly dangerous, however, was not the quake itself. If it had taken place in a rural area, it would not have caused so much destruction. But the epicenter was only about ten miles (16 km) from Port-au-Prince and its nearly 3 million residents living and working in buildings that had not been built to withstand the force. It was a recipe for disaster.

NOT OVER YET

Earthquakes are over in a matter of seconds, but they have aftershocks that can go on for quite some time.

History's Largest Quake

The strongest earthquake ever recorded was in Chile on May 22, 1960. It measured a magnitude 9.5. It killed approximately 1,655 people and left 2 million others homeless. The quake triggered tsunamis that killed 61 people in Hawaii and 138 people in Japan and left 32 people dead or missing in the Philippines.

Aftershocks are smaller tremors that follow a larger earthquake, also called a mainshock. In the four weeks following the January 12 mainshock, Haiti experienced 59 aftershocks of magnitude 4.5 or greater. Sixteen of those measured magnitudes of 5.0 or greater. The two strongest aftershocks were a magnitude 6.0 that occurred seven minutes after the mainshock, and a magnitude 5.9 that occurred January 20.

The earthquake also set off a tsunami. Tsunamis are strong sea waves that happen in response to seismic events such as earthquakes or volcanic eruptions. They can be very destructive when they reach shore. Several locations in Haiti and the Dominican Republic reported tsunamis after the quake, including the small Haitian fishing town of Petit Paradis. Four people were killed when they were washed out to sea with that wave.

Deadly Wave

On December 26, 2004, a massive earthquake measuring magnitude 9.1 occurred off the northern coast of the island of Sumatra. The quake triggered a massive tsunami that killed almost 230,000 people in 14 countries of South Asia and East Africa.

A collage of newspaper clippings tells of Haiti's struggle because of the earthquake.

Unlike weather disasters such as tornadoes or hurricanes, it is not possible to predict earthquakes, except by looking at history. Quakes along the Enriquillo-Plantain Garden Fault are not frequent. This section of Haiti might not experience another major earthquake for 100 years. The Caribbean is seismically very active, however. Jian Lin, a senior scientist with the Woods Hole Oceanographic

Institution, suggested other countries in the region take a lesson from Haiti. This quake was strong, shallow, and close to a densely populated— and poorly built—area. That made it a worst-case scenario. Lin said, "It should be a wake-up call for the entire Caribbean."[2]

The earthquake that hit Haiti was strong, but in an area with better building codes and stronger structures, it would not have done so much damage. In 1989, an earthquake hit the densely populated San Francisco Bay area in California. Twelve thousand people were left homeless and 63 were killed. The magnitude of that earthquake was 7.1—almost the same as the quake in Haiti. "Earthquakes don't kill people," says John Mutter, a seismologist and disaster expert at Columbia University. "Bad buildings kill people. And buildings are bad because people are poor."[3]

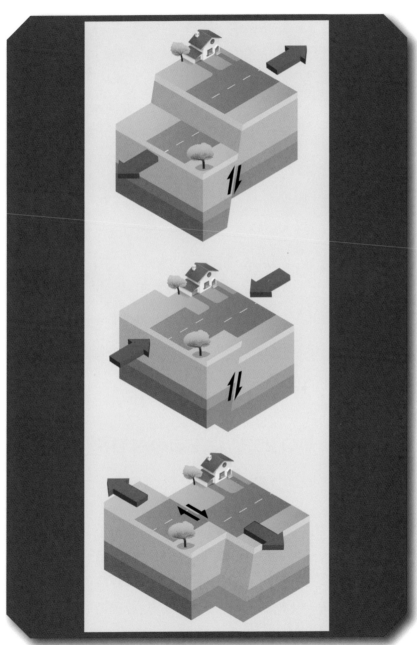

At fault lines, plates can move apart, push together, or slide against each other.

Haitian school children

Forty Seconds
of Horror

It was about 4:50 on the afternoon of
January 12. Stephanie and Rosemary
Pierre, cousins and classmates at the Andre Malraux
School in Port-au-Prince, were headed to class.
Romelus Daniel, Rosemary's boyfriend, walked with

them up the hill to the high school. Stephanie, 21, loved math and hoped to become a doctor. National exams were coming up, and she was determined to get into college. Maybe she was eager to start studying, or maybe she did not want to overhear the argument that Rosemary and Romelus were having, but when they got to the school, Stephanie headed right inside. As Rosemary and Romelus lingered outside, the ground began to shake. Before either of them realized what was happening, the school collapsed. "The argument, by the grace of God, saved me," said Rosemary.[1] Her cousin Stephanie, and many thousands of other Haitians, however, did not survive.

No Place to Hide

The earthquake began on the Enriquillo-Plantain Garden Fault, just 15 miles (24 km) from Haiti's densely populated capital city. The damage stretched across all of southwest Haiti. The epicenter was

The National Palace

Several palaces have been built on the site where the Haiti National Palace, or Presidential Palace, now lies in ruins. Each structure was damaged or destroyed in an effort to topple or assassinate a president. One palace was wrecked during a revolt in 1869. It was rebuilt in 1881 and then damaged in an explosion in 1912. A new palace was designed, but it was damaged by fire before it was finished. The current palace was completed in 1920.

A collapsed school in Haiti

nearest to the city of Léogâne, which was about 90 percent destroyed. The earthquake's tremors toppled buildings in Port-au-Prince, Petit-Goâve, Léogâne, and Jacmel. The death toll was particularly high in Port-au-Prince. Tremors from the quake were felt as far away as Cuba and Jamaica.

When the first tremors hit, buildings swayed back and forth. People driving had to fight to keep their cars on the road. In churches, the bells rang one last time before the steeples fell. Cheap concrete walls cracked and crumbled, sending clouds of dust into the air. Buildings "pancaked" on themselves, stacking the roofs and floors on top of each other, crushing everything and everyone inside. A witness described it, saying, "All of a sudden everything was just falling apart . . . there was no place to hide."[2]

People were trapped everywhere inside what used to be buildings. Some were still alive, but many were dead. Arms and legs stuck out from beneath piles of rubble, coated with blood, dirt, and concrete dust. Survivors worked with their bare hands to move the debris, calling out and listening for sounds and signs of life from within.

Whole neighborhoods collapsed. The streets flooded with people, bleeding, crying, dazed, and in shock. Some neighborhoods were entirely wiped from the hillsides around the city. Public buildings caved in, and schools

Search and Rescue

Teams of search and rescue dogs from all over the world were on hand to help in Haiti. China, Russia, Mexico, Peru, the United States, and dozens of other nations sent teams with canines to sniff out victims trapped deep in piles of rubble. A border collie named Hunter and his highly trained nose found three girls who were trapped under the remains of a four-story building.

and government buildings fell, trapping thousands inside.

Landmarks and symbols of Haiti's national heritage, such as the Presidential Palace and Port-au-Prince Cathedral were not spared. Nor were important government structures, such as the National Assembly, or parliament building, the Port-au-Prince city hall, and a number of ministry buildings. The quake did serious damage to the main prison, freeing some 4,000 of Haiti's most dangerous criminals and adding to the city's fear and misery.

Basic services, which were never very reliable to begin with, were lost. Electricity and telephone lines were knocked out as a result of the earthquake. Some cellular telephone service was available, but with so many people trying to call in and out, the system was overloaded. Experts recommended text messaging instead. This form of communication takes up less of the system's capacity, so it was more efficient than making a call.

Port-au-Prince Cathedral

Cathédrale Notre-Dame de L'Assomption, or the Cathedral of Our Lady of the Assumption, was another historic structure that was destroyed in the earthquake. This symbol of national pride took 30 years to build, from 1884 to 1914. Before it was destroyed, the cupolas, or domes, on its towers served as lighthouses for ships in the harbor.

In only 40 seconds, Haiti, a country that had already been through so much, had become a disaster area and was in agony.

No One Was Spared

It is horribly ironic that the quake nearly destroyed some of the organizations that would have been best able to help. The UN mission headquarters in the Christopher Hotel was reduced to rubble, and almost everyone inside was killed. In total, the UN lost 96 staff members, including Mission Chief Hédi Annabi and Deputy Luiz Carlos da Costa. It was the largest single loss of life in the history of UN peacekeeping.

The quake also dealt a terrible blow to the country's already-struggling medical system. Hospitals were severely damaged, including all three of the facilities run by Médecins Sans Frontières (MSF). The buildings became unsafe and unusable when they would be needed most. Stefano Zannini, head of the MSF mission in Haiti, described what he found as he worked through the night: "The situation [was] chaotic... I visited five medical centers, including a major hospital, and most of them were not functioning."[3]

These issues did not stop people from coming, however. In the first hours after the quake, hundreds of people streamed to hospitals and clinics, desperate for help. They carried loved ones on anything that would work as a stretcher, such as a sheet or an old door. They made splints for broken bones out of anything they could find—broken furniture, license plates from cars. The doctors did what they could, but many quake survivors had severe fractures, head injuries, and crushed arms

Doctors Without Borders

Médecins Sans Frontières (MSF) is also known as Doctors Without Borders. It is a humanitarian organization that provides medical aid to people whose survival is threatened by crisis situations, such as wars, epidemics, and natural disasters. MSF works independently of any government. Though the organization frequently works in war zones, it does not take sides in armed conflicts. Nearly all of MSF's funding comes from private sources. This is important, because it allows MSF to stay neutral and not be influenced by political, business, or religious groups.

Similarly, MSF's decision to treat any patient is made only on the basis of medical need. It does not discriminate on the basis of race, political considerations, or religious beliefs. MSF currently has 27,000 individuals at work in nearly 70 countries to make medical help available to anyone who needs it. In addition to providing medical services, MSF is committed to speaking out about injustice, abuse, and mistreatment anywhere in the world.

MSF was founded in 1971 by French doctors and journalists. Its members are all volunteers, and it has support offices in 19 countries located throughout the world. In 1999, MSF was awarded the Nobel Peace Prize for its humanitarian work.

or legs. All of these injuries would require surgery to repair, but in the first few hours, the medical teams did not have what they needed. There was some help, as members of Argentina's UN force evacuated gravely injured people to Santo Domingo in helicopters.

NEIGHBORS HELPING NEIGHBORS

Many survivors had little faith that any help would come. Violaine Bernardin lost her family and her home. She summed up the frustration that many Haitians felt: "I don't need anything. I lost my children . . . The government will do nothing. In Haiti, they never do anything."[4]

Others did what they could to help anyone in need. Juilie Exile brought a neighbor's child to what remained of the general hospital. The boy's father was dead, and with no official help coming, she and her neighbors dug the baby out of the rubble. "It's only neighbors helping neighbors," she said.[5]

DARKNESS FALLS

Aftershocks rocked the country for hours after the main quake. All around, the city's buildings continued to crumble and fall throughout the night,

A Landmark Unharmed

The impressive Citadelle Laferrière stands on a mountaintop in northeast Haiti, near the town of Milot. It was built after the revolution to provide protection in case of an attack by French forces. Construction began in 1805, but the huge stone fort was never completed. Though it has been damaged in the past by acts of nature, this piece of history was untouched by this latest earthquake.

injuring and frightening survivors. Those who had flashlights continued to dig. In the dark, fear spread with rumors of tsunamis, gangs, and more shaking.

With no electricity, no streetlights, and limited communications, the darkness was alive with the cries of the trapped and the mourning of the survivors. Structures and lives were devastated. Help was needed fast if Haiti was going to begin the process of recovery.

Collapsed homes in Port-au-Prince

The earthquake in Haiti resulted in massive destruction.

HELPING HANDS

I n the days following the January 12, 2010, earthquake in Haiti, the world looked on in horror as the news brought images of the destruction and death. With the loss of many of its buildings, and the deaths of several officials, the

Haitian government was paralyzed for several days. On January 15, government operations relocated to a building near the airport. In addition, the government gave control of the airport in Port-au-Prince to the United States to facilitate relief efforts transported by aircraft.

As the Haitian government scrambled to organize itself, governments, individuals, and aid organizations around the globe went into action. The UN World Food Programme (WFP) prepared to ship huge amounts of emergency rations. The United States sent a hospital ship, the USNS *Comfort*, and ordered marines and rescue teams to Haiti. A cell phone fundraising program started by the American Red Cross raised $8 million in a matter of days. The Red Cross estimated that 3 million people would need aid. Great Britain, Canada, China, Cuba, France, Germany, Mexico, and Venezuela also pledged aid and supplies. Many more countries would be added to the list in the coming days.

Miracle Survivor

Fifteen days after the quake struck, people combing through the rubble of their Carrefour-Feuilles district home heard a small voice. When they looked more closely, they were amazed to find a teenage girl still alive. Darlene Etienne had survived under remains of a house by drinking water from a bath. When she was finally found, rescuers determined that she might have survived only a few more hours.

GETTING IN

There was no shortage of help, but getting it to Haiti would prove to be a challenge. Shipping into Port-au-Prince was impossible for the first weeks following the disaster. The main port was so badly damaged that the U.S. Coast Guard deemed it unusable. By January 20, international aid ships were using it regardless of the Coast Guard's determination. Supplies simply had to get to the hardest-hit areas as quickly as possible.

Sending supplies by air was also challenging. Getting planes in was hampered by damage to the control tower at Toussaint L'Ouverture International Airport, outside of Port-au-Prince. The U.S. Air Force had been granted temporary control of the airport the day after the quake and had begun round-the-clock airlifts of water, medicine, and supplies. The air traffic was much heavier than what the airport had been built to handle. With only one runway, it was a challenge to get the dozens of aid flights in and out. At first, there was not enough fuel on hand. Planes that were allowed to land could not be refueled to leave again. Pilots had to circle the airport—sometimes for hours—waiting for a chance to land. In many cases, the planes were redirected to

A parcel of medicine boxes reading "Haiti Earthquake" is seen at the warehouse of Médecins Sans Frontiéres in Merignac, France, on January 14, 2010.

secondary airports or to the Dominican Republic. From there, the problem became how to get the aid and supplies into the areas where they were needed most. Many of the roads were destroyed or blocked with debris.

The United States did what it could with the airport's limited capabilities, but the commanders were criticized for the delays. MSF flights carrying desperately needed medical supplies and an inflatable hospital were turned away from the airport five times. Eventually, they had to land in the Dominican Republic.

DIGGING OUT

While organizations the world over scrambled to get aid into Haiti, the Haitian people scrambled to dig out. Seventy percent of Port-au-Prince lay in ruins. Almost all of Léogâne, which was closer to the epicenter of the quake, had fallen. In Jacmel, 20 to 30 percent of the buildings were destroyed. Everywhere, people worked to find loved ones in the remains of houses. Rescuers knew buried victims would likely not be alive. Still, they had to try and searched for several days.

Electronic Aid

Social networking played a huge part in the earthquake response. On Web sites such as Twitter and Facebook, the story of the earthquake unfolded in real time. Bloggers were also important for getting the word out. Missionary Troy Livesay kept his readers up to date by posting whenever he could. "I do not know why my house stands and my children all lie sleeping in their beds right now," he wrote. "It defies logic . . . my babies were spared while thousands of others were not."[1]

Social media was also an important factor in fundraising. Texting and Twitter were especially helpful to a campaign by the Red Cross. Cell phone users could donate $10 to Haiti relief efforts just by sending a text message that said "Haiti" to a specified number. Between January 12 and January 14, 2.3 million tweets contained the words *Red Cross* or *Haiti*. Almost 190,000 more contained the number to text. Thanks, in part, to the efforts of Twitter users, awareness of the texting campaign was increased, and the Red Cross raised $8 million by Friday, January 15.

Others used similar approaches to fundraising. Haitian-born musician Wyclef Jean also launched a texting campaign, asking his 1.4 million followers on Twitter to donate by texting. He raised $2 million.

In some cases, cell phones turned out to be life preservers. The Dominican Institute of Communications helped to restore Haiti's cellular services by arranging for a satellite link to replace damaged cell towers. Some lucky people were able to send text messages out and tell family members where they were trapped. A Canadian woman trapped under rubble sent a text message to the Foreign Affairs Office in Ottawa, Canada, some 1,900 miles (3,056 km) away. She told them where she was and that she was safe. The message was relayed to Canadian diplomats in Haiti, who arranged for her rescue. Others had to wait and hope to be found.

MEDICAL CHALLENGES

For many, being found in the ruins was only the first part of the struggle. Getting to a hospital was no guarantee of aid. Hospitals set up triage centers in parking lots and on sidewalks. There, they would have to decide who could be helped, who needed to be sent to a better facility, and who was beyond hope.

Medical care for earthquake victims was available and waiting in facilities beyond Haiti. Hospitals in the Dominican Republic and the United States were

Volunteers operate a makeshift medical clinic in Haiti.

standing by to care for the people who were severely injured but strong enough to travel. Still, in the coming weeks, many more would perish from their injuries.

BURYING THE DEAD

The parking lot of Port-au-Prince's main hospital became an unofficial morgue. Hundreds of dead bodies stacked up as people left behind loved ones who did not survive long enough to get to a doctor. Throughout the hardest-hit cities, bodies lay in the streets. In the Canape Vert neighborhood, men dug a large grave and buried the bodies of 31 family members. They knew no help was coming, and they were afraid the bodies were a health hazard to survivors. Eventually, the government began using bulldozers and dump trucks to collect and remove the dead. It is estimated that as many as 70,000 people were buried in mass graves.

Making Do

For survivors, immediate needs of clean drinking water, food, and safe shelter were becoming desperate. In some areas of Port-au-Prince, water was never reliably available. Where aid was slow in coming, some residents were fortunate enough to find springs of water coming from pipes that were damaged by the earthquake. The WFP brought in emergency rations, but distributing them fairly was a difficult task. At some distribution sites, mobbing crowds made it impossible and even dangerous to hand out supplies. In other places, aid organizations simply dropped packages from helicopters into open areas to avoid conflicts.

The quake left more than 1 million people homeless. All over destroyed cities, people made tents by tying tarps to trees or what was left of walls. They stretched sheets over poles or across anything that would give them a little shelter. Even those whose houses were still standing stayed outside and slept in the street. They feared that the weakened walls would come down with the tremor of an aftershock.

USNS *Comfort*

The United States Naval Ship *Comfort* is a hospital ship equipped with 12 operating rooms and 1,000 beds. It has been deployed to Iraq as well as to the U.S. Gulf Coast to assist with medical needs after hurricanes Katrina and Rita in 2005. It is a fully equipped hospital. About the only things the medical crew of the *Comfort* cannot do are organ transplants and open heart surgery. In addition, the ship has four distilling plants that can create 300,000 gallons (1,135,624 L) of clean, drinkable water per day.

In the wealthy suburb of Pétionville, a golf course became a village of thousands of tents. Twelve days after the quake, there were 25,000 people at the camp, nicknamed the Country Club. There were even shops in the tent-village. One woman was selling wigs and hair weaves, and a man was using a little generator and charging cell phones for customers. The camp was being run by Catholic Relief Services. Though it was quite well organized compared to some of the other places, there were problems with overcrowding and violence. Without toilets, there was human waste in the open, which created health hazards.

The Port-au-Prince police force lost as many as half of its officers in the quake. This loss, combined with the losses to other forces in the nation, made security difficult. With so many people living on the street, reports of prisoners escaping because the jail had been destroyed created great concern about safety. Stores and homes that had not been completely destroyed became targets for looters. Police were not able to tell whether the looters were dangerous criminals or just people desperate for food. In some cases, looters were shot and killed by the police, adding to the quake's tragedies.

Hope in the Rubble

Lemark Aristide, his father, and his baby brother were lucky. When their house fell, no one was killed. "A concrete block fell onto my legs," recalled Lemark. "I couldn't move and I was in pain."[2] Once he recovered from his shock, Lemark's father took stock of the situation. He and his infant son were also trapped, but through the darkness, he could see a ray of light coming from outside. Neighbors helped Mr. Aristide get out, and then they went to work to free Lemark. It took four more hours, but Lemark's good luck continued. A church pastor had a car and was able to drive the Aristides to the town of Fond Parisien. There, doctors put Lemark in a cast from the hips down, saving his life.

Maximillien François lost a great deal when the quake hit. His father, his only brother, and his cousin were all killed in a collapsed building. Max was trapped when his leg was crushed under a fallen wall. There were no functioning hospitals near his home, but there was a convoy going to the Dominican Republic. Max and his mother were taken to Santo Domingo. Doctors feared they would have to amputate Max's leg. After an operation, however, they were hopeful that they had saved it and that he might be able to play soccer again soon. Max would have to adjust to his new physical state and focus on healing. This would be the challenge for all Haitians.

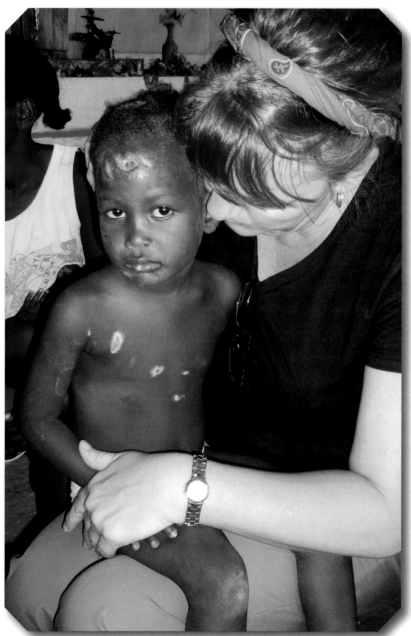

Many Haiti earthquake victims were children.

Andre Chandle, 13, suffered a head injury as a result of the earthquake. He survived with the help of medical volunteers.

ADJUSTING TO A NEW LIFE

A fter any disaster, there comes a point when authorities have to make a difficult decision: when to stop searching for survivors. Ten days after the earthquake, on January 22, 2010, the Haitian government officially called off the search. Even if they had survived the quake, after that amount of time, anyone still trapped under the rubble would have died. There were miraculous stories of people who were rescued after January 22, but they were few in number. Rather than continuing to focus on searching for what would now be bodies, the government had to concentrate its resources on helping the living.

MEDICAL PROGRESS

In the weeks after the quake, medical professionals from all over the world volunteered to go to Haiti to help. With those volunteers and with the efforts of organizations such as Médecins Sans Frontières (MSF) and the International Red Cross, Haiti's health care system got a much-needed boost. At the beginning of 2010, MSF was operating four health care facilities in Port-au-Prince.

Unhealthy Situation

Health concerns caused by the Haiti earthquake were pressing in the days following the disaster. Without homes and proper sanitation, everyone was at risk, especially the youngest Haitians. Pierre Biales is a French psychologist working with the Red Cross. In late January 2010, he was busy counseling earthquake victims and teaching basic hygiene to children living in camps. He explained how people were living in the streets, sleeping there, and using them in place of bathrooms, which were few and far between. Biales said of the situation, "Their parents are sad because they have lost children, friends or family members. Taking care of the children is now an emergency."[1]

Inflatable Hospitals

Médecins Sans Fron-
tières (Doctors Without
Borders) has been using
tentlike temporary medi-
cal facilities for a number
of years. The inflatable
hospitals are made of the
same material as inflat-
able lifeboats. They come
in bundles about the size
of a desk, which are then
unfolded on a type of rub-
ber mat that acts as a floor
and connected to an air
pump. It takes 30 to 36
hours to assemble a hos-
pital the size of a football
field. Once it is inflated,
the pillars inside feel as
sturdy as concrete.

By May, that number had increased
to 20, along with four mobile
clinics. During the four months
following the earthquake, MSF
treated nearly 137,000 patients and
performed close to 8,000 surgeries.
In addition, the organization worked
to keep people healthy by giving out
28,000 tents and building
800 latrines.

Immediately after the quake,
doctors focused on emergency
care, triage, and lifesaving surgery.
Later, the focus changed. People
needed ongoing care to recover from
surgeries and amputations. Doctors
had to make sure these patients did
not develop infections that would
add more deaths to the quake's toll.
And other health issues that existed before the quake
continued, including a lower life expectancy than
the United States (61 years compared to 78) and a
mortality rate for pregnant woman that is 50 times
higher than in the United States. Doctors were kept
extremely busy helping people with other illnesses

and psychological needs due to the trauma of the quake. They were also delivering babies and caring for new mothers, many of whom were now homeless.

SEARCHING FOR THE CHILDREN

The earthquake left many children orphaned and on their own. To locate their parents or other family members, in February 2010, the United Nations Children's Fund (UNICEF) began working to compile a registry of children who were orphaned or separated from their parents.

Marie de la Soudière is a child-protection specialist with UNICEF and coordinator of the registry program.

Trafficking or Rescuing?

On January 29, 2010, ten missionaries from Ohio were arrested as they tried to take a busload of 33 children from Haiti into the Dominican Republic. The missionaries claimed that the children, ages 2 through 12, were orphans. The children were not orphans. Within three weeks of the group's arrest, parents for all but one child were located.

This case highlighted something that had worried Haitian officials since the day of the earthquake. Child trafficking was a problem in Haiti long before the 2010 earthquake, but now, Haiti's children seemed to be even more at risk.

What makes this case difficult to judge is that most of the missionaries truly seemed to think they were doing good work. They claimed that all they wanted to do was give the children better lives than they could have in Haiti. Haitian authorities must have believed them. By April 27, 2010, all but the leader of the group had been freed.

Her motto is "No to orphanages."[2] The earthquake made Haiti's children even more vulnerable to child trafficking. La Soudière is certain the registry—and detective work—will help keep Haitian children with their families.

LEAVING PORT-AU-PRINCE

Something that could make La Soudière's job harder is that many people fled the Port-au-Prince area after the earthquake. They headed for other parts of the country—some to stay with family members, some just to live in another tent in a different city. All of them felt safer out of the quake zone and off of the streets of Port-au-Prince. The government encouraged people to relocate away from the city, which was far too crowded even before the quake. In fact, the government discouraged people from coming back at all. Instead, its vision for rebuilding Haiti means spreading out the population.

Some Haitians left their homeland altogether. Eleven-year-old Madjany Mouscardy went to live with a relative in Miramar, Florida. One month after the quake, she was enrolled in a new school a world away from the destruction in Haiti. But it will

Christine Jennifer Delma, left, *and Sebastien Emile,* below right, *moved from Haiti to the United States after the January 2010 earthquake.*

never be possible for her to forget January 12. When the tremor hit, she was buried in a hole, surrounded by concrete blocks. "I couldn't breathe," she said. "But I said to myself, 'Madjany, you are not going to die.' And then I started to lift the bricks off me until I could see blue sky."[3]

Madjany had to leave her parents behind in Haiti, but they were still alive. Garvey Fils-Amie, also 11, was not so fortunate. With his mother dead, he moved to Miramar to start a new life with his uncle. Garvey and Madjany are not alone. They are only two of the more than 2,000 Haitian children now enrolled in schools across all of Florida. These children have each other to rely on for understanding and cultural connection. And they have teachers, relatives, and other adults to go to for support.

WATCHING FOR THE RAINS

By April 2010, a great deal of progress had been made in Haiti. Looking ahead, however, everyone was nervous. Haiti's rainy season usually begins in April and is followed by the hurricane season. Authorities and aid organizations were concerned that people living in tents would be in danger of drowning in the floods and mudslides that often come with the rains. Doctors were concerned that diseases such as malaria and typhoid fever could spread.

The government knew from the first day after the quake that the rainy season would bring more trouble to the victims. In the first weeks after the quake, however, the biggest concerns were simply for survival. It took time to establish a system of

Refugees sought shelter in Corail-Cesselesse.

registering citizens in the various camps and tent
cities. It also took time to find a more suitable place
for them to stay.

One such place was a camp called Corail-
Cesselesse. Located approximately nine miles
(14 km) north of Port-au-Prince, it was built with
the combined efforts of the United States, the UN,
and the Haitian government. On April 10, the first
thousands of homeless people were transferred to
Corail-Cesselesse from the camp at the Pétionville
golf course. There, they would have sturdier shelters
and better sanitation. To avoid the rains, people

"With Katrina, if you could walk to the edge of a disaster area, you could get in a car, drive 40 miles, find a store and buy what you needed. Here, there is no car. There is no highway. There is no 40 miles away."[6]

—*Caryl Stern, president of the U.S. Fund for UNICEF*

would have to be moved quickly. In fact, Haitian President Préval was criticized for moving families to the camp before it was really ready—the decision was deemed hasty and ill-planned. The latrines were barely in place before the first arrivals. "We have to confront all the problems at the same time," he said, "because the rainy season is coming and not only to Port-au-Prince."[4]

The Corail-Cesselesse relocation effort was made quickly, without the opportunity for much preparation, but workers did what they could. Marcel Stoessel of Oxfam, a relief organization, explained the situation: "We realise [sic] this is an emergency relocation due to impending rains and we are moving with utmost urgency to prepare this site. But future moves cannot be done in this last-minute fashion."[5] Once the immediate needs of victims are met, the government faces an immense challenge: planning, preparing, and building for the future. Haiti must re-create itself and do a better job of it—to avoid such disasters in the future, and to simply become a stronger nation.

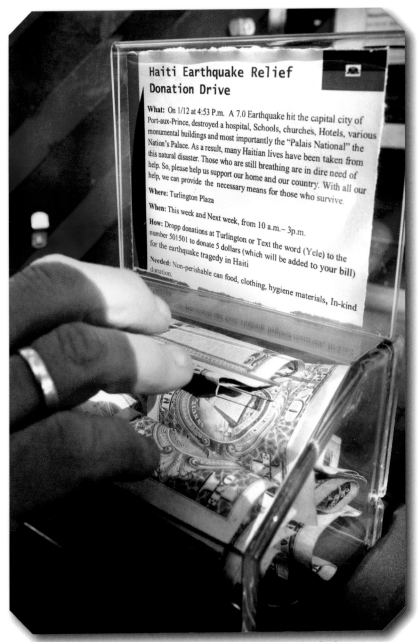

Haiti Earthquake Relief Donation Drive

What: On 1/12 at 4:53 P.m. A 7.0 Earthquake hit the capital city of Port-aux-Prince, destroyed a hospital, Schools, churches, Hotels, various monumental buildings and most importantly the "Palais National" the Nation's Palace. As a result, many Haitian lives have been taken from this natural disaster. Those who are still breathing are in dire need of help. So, please help us support our home and our country. With all our help, we can provide the necessary means for those who survive.

Where: Turlington Plaza

When: This week and Next week, from 10 a.m.– 3p.m.

How: Dropp donations at Turlington or Text the word (Yele) to the number 501501 to donate 5 dollars (which will be added to your bill) for the earthquake tragedy in Haiti

Needed: Non-perishable can food, clothing, hygiene materials, In-kind donation.

Haiti's recovery depends on support from individuals and governments worldwide.

Women march in Port-au-Prince on March 8, 2010, to commemorate International Women's Day. Their sign reads "Women will rebuild Haiti."

BUILDING BACK BETTER

Working with the UN and the World Bank, Haiti's government has estimated it will cost $11.5 billion and take three years to rebuild the country. The UN Food and Agriculture Organization (FAO) estimates it will cost

$800 million to revive Haiti's agriculture system. Haitian President Préval has noted it will take years just to remove the fallen buildings. He said, "It will take 1,000 trucks moving rubble for 1,000 days, so that's three years. And until we move out rubble, we cannot really build."[1]

PLEDGING SUPPORT

Numerous aid organizations have long been committed to working in Haiti, and after the earthquake, their numbers increased. In March, there were more than 10,000 humanitarian organizations at work in the nation.

On March 31, 2010, the United States and the UN, in cooperation with the government of Haiti, hosted the International Donors' Conference Towards a New Future for Haiti. Its goal was to generate international financial support for Haiti's redevelopment. Haiti requested $3.8 billion in the next 18 months to meet its short-term needs. Forty-eight countries pledged to give a collective $9.9 billion. That included $5.3 billion for the next 18 months, which far exceeded Haiti's request.

In addition to promises of support, many nations have also agreed to forgive debts owed to them by

Haiti. Canada, the United States, the United Kingdom (UK), France, Germany, Italy, and Japan pledged to forgive Haiti's loans, and the World Bank is considering forgiving $38 million in loans. This freed up money Haiti needs to rebuild. "It must be right that a nation buried in rubble must not also be buried in debt," declared UK Prime Minister Gordon Brown.[2]

BLUEPRINTS FOR RECOVERY

At the International Donors' Conference, Haiti unveiled a 55-page plan for rebuilding. The plan's central idea is to spread out the huge population of Port-au-Prince into smaller cities around the country. Limiting the concentration of people in one city will help keep more Haitians at a safer distance from another natural disaster. It will also help spread government aid to other towns, such as Jacmel. As the country recovers, those smaller cities will become centers where Haitian people can find jobs and other opportunities. The government will also put new building codes in place to ensure that

Haiti's new cities are sturdier and more resistant to the destruction that earthquakes can cause. And government buildings will be spread out to strengthen government presence in the nation.

Of course, the plan calls for improvements to basic things, such as electrical and sewer systems, hospitals, and schools. It also calls for environmental improvements and agricultural support. Those changes will help relieve some of the poverty in Haiti's rural areas as well.

Experts believe the government's plan is a good one—even better than early plans for the recovery of New Orleans, Louisiana, after Hurricane Katrina.

Earthquake-proof Buildings?

Living, and rebuilding, in an earthquake zone mean taking building codes very seriously. Different construction techniques and technologies can increase the chance a building will survive if the ground underneath it should shake.

There are two ways to think about earthquake-proofing a building: make it stronger, or make it more flexible. Low, square buildings tend to be more stable. Using high-quality concrete and reinforcing it with steel rods will also make walls stronger.

Skyscrapers and other tall buildings usually need to be more flexible. Many skyscraper designs use what is called "base isolation." With base isolation, the building and the foundation are separate. The building sits on a system of ball bearings or springs, so that if the ground moves, the building's base can move, and the rest of the building will stay where it is. The building might sway a little, but only very little. Most important, it will not crumble with the shock of the quake. High-tech buildings are more expensive, however, and no structure can be completely earthquake-proof.

Workers got to work rebuilding Haiti beginning in April 2010.

In order for the plan to work, the countries that
pledged support will have to fulfill their promises.
However, any improvements in Haiti will require
major changes to Haiti's government.

MORE THAN MONEY

Although there had been improvements made in
Haiti's government in recent years, the January 2010
earthquake showed the world that Haiti's government
is still unable to meet the needs of its people. The
republic's legacy of poverty and political corruption
made this natural disaster far worse than it had to

be. If Haiti is to recover, it will have to rebuild more than its cities. Haiti will have to create a government that can be trusted.

Once immediate needs of food and shelter are met, larger problems must be addressed. Before the quake, Haiti's medical system was inadequate. In its ruined state, that system is completely overwhelmed— and it will be for a long time to come. And once hospitals are rebuilt, the country will need local professionals to staff them.

The rebuilding of Haiti will also require overhauling the nation's school system. Without opportunities for education, Haiti will never be able to train the doctors, teachers, scientists, and other professionals it needs for long-term recovery and growth. And the latest disaster has meant many children have lost their chance for education. That could threaten the country's long-term recovery.

Haiti has a long history of governments working against their citizens rather than for them. In response, Haitian citizens work around the government, rather than with it. Until they are able to work with each other, any progress will be slow at best. Disaster experts have noted that Haiti needs a strong economy and a trustworthy government able

Global Perspective

At the International Donor's Conference, U.S. Secretary of State Hillary Clinton reported on the levels of aid flowing into Haiti. "To put this effort in perspective," she said, "after the (Indian Ocean) tsunami, more than 80 countries provided immediate humanitarian assistance, and more than 20 countries pledged assistance for reconstruction. As of today, more than 140 countries have provided humanitarian assistance to Haiti, and nearly 50 countries have made pledges of support for Haiti's rebuilding."[6]

to function without outside help once international aid runs out. "Aid is important but aid has never saved a country," said U.S. Secretary of State Hillary Clinton. "Our goal must be the empowerment of the Haitian people. They're the ones who will carry on the work of rebuilding Haiti long after our involvement has ended."[4]

Given Haiti's location, it is certain to experience more natural disasters. Hurricanes are a fact of life for the Caribbean. Without a strong new foundation, another year similar to 2008 will bring much more destruction and misery. It is possible to build structures—and governments—that can withstand natural disasters. That is what must happen in Haiti now. "It would be unconscionable [unjust] to turn Port-au-Prince back to the way it was," says seismologist and disaster expert John Mutter. "You have to use this as a perverse chance to build back better."[5]

Haitians' faith and determination will help them recover from the devastating earthquake of 2010.

TIMELINE

1492	1697	1791
On December 5, Christopher Columbus first sees the island now known as Hispaniola.	The Treaty of Ryswick divides Hispaniola between Spain and France.	A bloody slave revolt marks the beginning of a revolution that will eventually end French rule.

1915	1957	1971
U.S. marines land in Haiti on July 28, beginning an occupation that will last until 1934.	François "Papa Doc" Duvalier wins the presidential election and later declares himself president for life.	François Duvalier dies on April 21. Jean-Claude "Baby Doc" Duvalier takes over as president for life.

1804

On January 1, Jean-Jacques Dessalines declares Saint-Domingue free from French rule. The new country is called Haiti.

1825

France officially recognizes the Haitian republic.

1825

Haiti begins paying millions of francs to France for losses from the revolution.

1986

Jean-Claude Duvalier flees to France on February 7.

1990

On December 16, Jean-Bertrand Aristide is the first democratically elected president of Haiti.

1991

Aristide is removed from office in an army coup led by Raoul Cédras on September 30.

TIMELINE

1994	1995	2001
Aristide is reinstated as president in October.	Réne Préval is elected president, but it is widely believed Aristide continues to have power.	Aristide is elected president again.

2010	2010	2010
On January 12, a 7.0 earthquake strikes Haiti, killing an estimated 230,000 people and leaving another 1.5 million homeless.	Between January 12 and 14, people worldwide text donations of some $8 million to the Red Cross for Haiti relief.	The United States takes temporary control of Haiti's airport on January 15 to help the relief process.

2004

After bloody protests against his presidency, Aristide goes into exile.

2006

Réne Préval is elected president a second time.

2008

Haiti is devastated by a series of three hurricanes and a tropical storm that kill 800 people.

2010

On January 22, Haitian government officials call off the search for earthquake survivors.

2010

Canada, the United States, the United Kingdom, France, Germany, Italy, and Japan pledge in February to forgive Haiti's loans.

2010

An 8.8 earthquake in Chile on February 27 highlights Haiti's lack of resources and earthquake preparedness.

Essential Facts

Date of Event

January 12, 2010

Place of Event

Léogâne, Port-au-Prince, and Jacmel, Haiti

Key Players

❖ Toussaint L'Ouverture

❖ François "Papa Doc" Duvalier

❖ Jean-Claude "Baby Doc" Duvalier

❖ Jean-Bertrand Aristide

❖ Réne Préval

❖ Médecins Sans Frontières (Doctors Without Borders)

❖ United Nations

❖ Numerous governments and relief organizations worldwide

Highlights of Event

❖ An earthquake struck Haiti's most densely populated areas on January 12, 2010. The cities of Port-au-Prince and Léogâne were almost completely destroyed. Poorly constructed buildings collapsed, immediately causing tens of thousands of deaths and leaving more than 1 million people homeless.

❖ After years of corruption and poverty, the nation of Haiti was ill-equipped to handle a massive natural disaster on the heels of hurricane devastation.

❖ The world immediately responded with aid, including millions of dollars in donations via text message from January 12 to 14.

❖ On January 15, Haiti's government gave temporary control of the airport to the United States to better manage relief efforts.

❖ The Haitian government officially ended the search for earthquake survivors on January 22.

❖ On March 31, the United Nations, the United States, and Haiti hosted the International Donors' Conference Towards a New Future in Haiti. The event focused on obtaining international financial support for Haiti's redevelopment.

Quote

"It would be unconscionable [unjust] to turn Port-au-Prince back to the way it was. You have to use this as a perverse chance to build back better."—*John Mutter, seismologist and disaster expert, Columbia University*

ADDITIONAL RESOURCES

SELECT BIBLIOGRAPHY

Coupeau, Steeve. *The History of Haiti.* Westport, CT: Greenwood, 2008.

Davis, Wade. *The Serpent and the Rainbow: A Harvard Scientist's Astonishing Journey into the Secret Societies of Haitian Voodoo, Zombis, and Magic.* New York: Simon & Schuster, 1997.

Diamond, Jared. *Collapse: How Societies Choose to Fail or Succeed.* New York: Penguin, 2005.

Heinl, Robert Debs, Jr., and Nancy Gordon Heinl. *Written in Blood: The Story of the Haitian People, 1492–1995.* Rev. ed. Lanham, MD: UP of America, 1996.

U.S. Department of the Interior/U.S. Geological Survey. *Earthquake Hazards Program.* 4 May 2010. 5 May 2010. <http://earthquake.usgs.gov/>.

Walsh, Bryan, Jay Newton-Small, and Tim Padgett. "Aftershock." *Time.* 1 Feb. 2010: 32.

FURTHER READING

Blashfield, Jean F. *Haiti: Enchantment of the World.* New York: Children's, 2008.

Goldish, Meish. *Crisis in Haiti.* Brookfield, CT: Millbrook, 1994.

Kusky, Timothy. *Earthquakes: Plate Tectonics and Earthquake Hazards.* New York: Facts on File, 2008.

Rockwell, Anne. *Open the Door to Liberty!: A Biography of Toussaint L'Ouverture.* Boston, MA: Houghton Mifflin, 2009.

Web Links

To learn more about the Haiti earthquake, visit ABDO Publishing Company online at **www.abdopublishing.com**. Web sites about the Haiti earthquake are featured on our Book Links page. These links are routinely monitored and updated to provide the most current information available.

Places To Visit

Haitian Heritage Museum
4141 NE Second Avenue, Suite 105C, Miami, FL 33137
305-371-5988
www.haitianheritagemuseum.org
The museum is dedicated to preserving the rich culture and heritage of Haiti through visual art, artifacts, music, film, and literature.

USGS Visitors Center
USGS Headquarters, 12201 Sunrise Valley Drive
Reston, VA 20192
703-648-4748
www.usgs.gov/visitors/
The U.S. Geological Survey (USGS) Learning Program introduces visitors to the work of the USGS and learning about natural science through guided tours and hands-on experiences.

GLOSSARY

aftershock
A smaller tremor that follows the main shock of an earthquake.

amputate
To surgically remove a limb from the body.

cacao
The beans used to make cocoa and chocolate.

convoy
A group of vehicles organized for efficient moving.

coup d'état
The violent overthrow of a government by a small group.

dictatorship
A type of government headed by a person or group that holds absolute power.

epicenter
The location on the earth's surface directly above where an earthquake started.

exile
To be forced to leave one's home country.

export
To sell or send something to another country.

fault
The line where the edges of tectonic plates meet.

hypocenter
The location on a fault below the earth's surface where an earthquake begins.

indigo
A valuable blue dye.

infrastructure
The system of public works, such as roads, sewers, and electrical service, for a region.

magnitude
> The size or intensity of an earthquake.

reparation
> Payment for damages.

seismology
> The study of earthquakes and other vibrations of the earth.

subsistence farming
> Farming that provides only enough food for the farming family.

successor
> A person who takes over an office or a title.

tectonic plates
> Massive plates that make up Earth's crust.

temblor
> An earthquake.

trafficking
> Illegally buying and selling.

triage
> Sorting and prioritizing patients.

tsunami
> A great sea wave usually associated with an earthquake.

vulnerable
> Easily damaged or injured.

Source Notes

Chapter 1. New Year's Hopes
1. Mike Clary. "Haitian children start over in Florida schools."
LATimes.com. 21 Feb. 2010. 5 May 2010
<http://www.latimes.com/news/nation-and-world/la-na-haitian-kids21-2010feb21,0,2276595.story>.

Chapter 2. Haiti's Early History
None.

Chapter 3. Haiti in the Twentieth Century
1. Robert Debs Heinl, Jr., and Nancy Gordon Heinl, Revised by
Michael Heinl. *Written in Blood: The Story of the Haitian People, 1492–1995*.
Lanham, MD: UP of America, 1996. 385.
2. Steve Coupeau. *The History of Haiti*. Westport, CT: Greenwood,
2008. 78.
3. Robert Debs Heinl, Jr., and Nancy Gordon Heinl, Revised by
Michael Heinl. *Written in Blood: The Story of the Haitian People, 1492–1995*.
Lanham, MD: UP of America, 1996. 577.
4. C. Michel and P. Bellegarde-Smith. *Vodou in Haitian Life and Culture:
Invisible Powers*. New York: Palgrave McMillan, 2006. 28.

Chapter 4. Haiti's Challenges
1. Haiti Micah Project. "Haiti Facts and Statistics." *Haiti-Micah.org*.
2006. 9 June 2010 <http://www.haiti-micah.org/
haiti-facts.html>.

Chapter 5. How Earthquakes Work
1. U.S. Department of the Interior/U.S. Geological Survey.
"Earthquakes, Megaquakes, and Disasters: Lights, Cameras,
Disaster!" *USGS.gov*. 12 Nov. 2009. 31 May 2010
<http://earthquake.usgs.gov/learn/topics/megaquakes.php>.
2. Woods Hole Oceanographic Institution. "News Release: WHOI
Expert: Haiti quake occurred in complex, active seismic region."
WHOI.edu. 2007. 5 May 2010 <http://www.whoi.edu/
page.do?pid=7545&tid=282&cid=66766&ct=162>.

3. Bryan Walsh, Jay Newton-Small, and Tim Padgett. "Aftershock." *Time.com.* 1 Feb. 2010. 7 May 2010. <http://www.time.com/time/specials/packages/article/0,28804,1953379_1953494_1955284,00.html>.

Chapter 6. Forty Seconds of Horror
1. William Booth and Scott Wilson. "Destruction of schools in Haiti quake crushes hopes of a better future for many." *WashingtonPost.com.* 23 Jan. 2010. 5 May 2010 <http://www.washingtonpost.com/wp-dyn/content/article/2010/01/22/AR2010012203476.html>.
2. "Haiti devastated by massive earthquake." *BBC.com.* 13 Jan. 2010. 5 May 2010 <http://news.bbc.co.uk/2/hi/8455629.stm>.
3. "Haiti: MSF Teams Set up Clinics to Treat Injured After Facilities Are Damaged." *DoctorsWithoutBorders.org.* 13 Jan. 2010. 5 May 2010 <http://www.doctorswithoutborders.org/news/article.cfm?id=4148&cat=field-news>.
4. Marisol Bello and John A. Torres. "Chaos in Haiti as rescue teams arrive." *USAToday.com.* 16 Jan. 2010. 5 May 2010 <http://www.usatoday.com/news/world/2010-01-13-Haiti-main_N.htm>.
5. Ibid.

Chapter 7. Helping Hands
1. Jim Kavanagh. "Family sends heartfelt reports from Haiti." *CNN.com.* 14 Jan. 2010. 31 May 2010. <http://www.cnn.com/2010/LIVING/01/14/haiti.bloggers.livesay/index.html>.
2. Jennifer Bakody. "A Haitian father's account of the earthquake and its aftermath." *UNICEF.org.* 19 Feb. 2010. 7 May 2010 <http://www.unicef.org/infobycountry/haiti_52806.html>.

SOURCE NOTES CONTINUED

Chapter 8. Adjusting to a New Life
1. Tom Phillips. "Haiti doctors fear malaria and typhoid as rainy season arrives." *The Observer Online*. 31 Jan. 2010. 7 May 2010 <http://www.guardian.co.uk/world/2010/jan/31/ haiti-disease-epidemics-earthquake>.
2. Tim Padgett and Jessica Desvarieux. "In Haiti, Aid Workers Help Orphans Find Relatives." *Time.com*. 8 Mar. 2010. 7 May 2010 <http://www.time.com/time/magazine/article/ 0,9171,1968109,00.html>.
3. Mike Clary. "Haitian children start over in Florida schools." *LATimes.com*. 21 Feb. 2010, 7 May 2010 <http://articles.latimes.com/2010/feb/21/nation/ la-na-haitian-kids21-2010feb21>.
4. "Haiti begins relocating quake victims ahead of rains." *BBC.com*. 11 Apr. 2010. 7 May 2010 <http://news.bbc.co.uk/2/hi/ americas/8614278.stm>.
5. Ibid.
6. Bryan Walsh, Jay Newton-Small, and Tim Padgett. "Aftershock." *Time.com*. 1 Feb. 2010. 7 May 2010 <http://www.time.com/time/ specials/packages/article/0,28804,1953379_1953494_1955284,00. html>.

Chapter 9. Building Back Better

1. Kirsten Johnson and Carolina Correa. "'It Will Take 1,000 Trucks 1,000 Days' to Clear Haiti's Rubble, Haiti's President Says." *CNSNews.com*. 16 Feb. 2010. 7 May 2010 <http://www.cnsnews.com/news/article/61390>.

2. "G7 nations pledge debt relief for quake-hit Haiti." *BBCNews.com*. 7 Feb. 2010. 7 May 2010 <http://news.bbc.co.uk/2/hi/8502567.stm>.

3. Ibid.

4. Michelle Nichols and Andrew Quinn. "Donors pledge millions for Haiti aid." *Reuters.com*. 31 Mar. 2010. 7 May 2010 <http://www.reuters.com/article/idUSN31203138>.

5. Bryan Walsh, Jay Newton-Small, and Tim Padgett. "Aftershock." *Time.com*. 1 Feb. 2010. 7 May 2010. <http://www.time.com/time/specials/packages/article/0,28804,1953379_1953494_1955284,00.html>.

6. "Haiti Donor Meeting Far Exceeds $4B Goal." *CBSNews.com*. 31 Mar. 2010. 7 May 2010 <http://www.cbsnews.com/stories/2010/03/31/world/main6350269.shtml>.

INDEX

ABOUT THE AUTHOR

Anne Lies is a writer and editor who works and lives in Minneapolis, Minnesota. She has a long background in education, including 12 years with the Minneapolis Public Schools and five years tutoring writers at Metropolitan State University in St. Paul, Minnesota. Anne has a bachelor's degree in writing and photography from Metropolitan State University. She is an avid gardener and urban farmer. During the long Minnesota winters, she likes to knit and dream about spring.

PHOTO CREDITS

HO/Reuters/Corbis, cover, title page; Niko Guido/iStockphoto, 6, 97; Ariana Cubillos/AP Images, 10, 56, 95; Gerald Herbert/ AP Images, 13, 99; Red Line Editorial, 14; AP Images, 16, 23, 27, 33, 96 ; Milos Peric/iStockphoto, 24; Toby Massey/AP Images, 29; Daniel Morel/AP Images, 35, 41; Steve Lindridge/iStockphoto, 36, 98 (top); Andres Leighton/AP Images, 38; Lynne Sladky/AP Images, 45; iStockphoto, 46; Claudia Dewald/iStockphoto, 50; Sherwin McGehee/iStockphoto, 53; iStockphoto, 55; A Growing Hope for Haiti, 58, 66, 72, 77, 98 (bottom); Esteban Felix/AP Images, 65, 78, 88; Bob Edme/AP Images, 69; Steven Senne/AP Images, 83; Ramon Espinosa, File/AP Images, 85; Doug Finger, The Gainesville Sun/AP Images, 87; Ramon Espinosa/AP Images, 92